CHILDREN'S CLASSICS
EVERYMAN'S LIBRARY

Hilaire Belloc

Cautionary
Verses

With illustrations
by B.T.B. and Nicolas Bentley

EVERYMAN'S LIBRARY
CHILDREN'S CLASSICS

First included in Everyman's Library 1997
Design and typography © David Campbell Publishers Ltd., 1997

Book design by Barbara de Wilde, Carol Devine Carson
and Peter B. Willberg

Five of Ernest H. Shepard's illustrations from *Dream Days* by Kenneth
Grahame are reprinted on the endpapers by permission of The Bodley
Head, London. The sixth illustration is by
S.C. Hulme Beaman

ISBN 1-85715-937-3

A CIP catalogue record for this book is available from the British Library

Published by David Campbell Publishers Ltd.,
79 Berwick Street, London W1V 3PF

Distributed by Random House (UK) Ltd.,
20 Vauxhall Bridge Road, London SW1V 2SA

Typeset by AccComputing, Castle Cary, Somerset

Printed and bound in Germany
by Graphischer Grossbetrieb Pössneck GmbH

CONTENTS

CAUTIONARY TALES FOR CHILDREN
Illustrated by B. T. B.

NEW CAUTIONARY TALES

Illustrated by Nicolas Bentley

THE BAD CHILD'S BOOK OF BEASTS

Illustrated by B. T. B.

MORE BEASTS FOR WORSE CHILDREN
Illustrated by B. T. B.

MORE PEERS

Illustrated by B. T. B.

A MORAL ALPHABET

Illustrated by B. T. B.

LADIES AND GENTLEMEN

Illustrated by Nicolas Bentley

CAUTIONARY TALES
FOR CHILDREN

INTRODUCTION

Upon being asked by a Reader whether the verses contained in this book were true.

And is it True? It is not True.
And if it were it wouldn't do,
For people such as me and you
Who pretty nearly all day long
Are doing something rather wrong.
Because if things were really so,
You would have perished long ago,
And I would not have lived to write
The noble lines that meet your sight,
Nor B. T. B. survived to draw
The nicest things you ever saw.

H. B.

Jim,

Who ran away from his Nurse, and was eaten by a Lion.

There was a Boy whose name was Jim;
His Friends were very good to him.
They gave him Tea, and Cakes, and Jam,
And slices of delicious Ham,
And Chocolate with pink inside,
And little Tricycles to ride,
And

   read him stories through and through,
And even took him to the Zoo –
But there it was the dreadful Fate
Befell him, which I now relate.

You know – at least you *ought* to know,
For I have often told you so –
That Children never are allowed
To leave their Nurses in a Crowd;

Now this was Jim's especial Foible,
He ran away when he was able,
And on this inauspicious day
He slipped his hand and ran away!
He hadn't gone a yard when –

Bang!
With open Jaws, a Lion sprang,
And hungrily began to eat
The Boy: beginning at his feet.

Now just imagine how it feels
When first your toes and then your heels,
And then by gradual degrees,
Your shins and ankles, calves and knees,
Are slowly eaten, bit by bit.

No wonder Jim detested it!
No wonder that he shouted "Hi!"
The Honest Keeper heard his cry,
Though very fat

           he almost ran
To help the little gentleman.
"Ponto!" he order as he came
(For Ponto was the Lion's name),
"Ponto!" he cried,

         with angry Frown.
"Let go, Sir! Down, Sir! Put it down!"

The Lion made a sudden Stop,
He let the Dainty Morsel drop,
And slunk reluctant to his Cage,
Snarling with Disappointed Rage
But when he bent him over Jim,
The Honest Keeper's

Eyes were dim.
The Lion having reached his Head,
The miserable Boy was dead!

When Nurse informed his parents, they
Were more Concerned than I can say: –
His Mother, as She dried her eyes,
Said, "Well – it gives me no surprise,
He would not do as he was told!"
His Father, who was self-controlled,
Bade all the children round attend

To James' miserable end,
And always keep a-hold of Nurse
For fear of finding something worse.

Henry King,

Who chewed bits of String, and was early cut off in Dreadful Agonies.

The Chief Defect of Henry King
Was

chewing little bits of String.
At last he swallowed some which tied

Itself in ugly Knots inside.

Physicians of the Utmost Fame
Were called at once; but when they came
They answered,

                as they took their Fees,
"There is no Cure for this Disease.
Henry will very soon be dead."
His parents stood about his Bed
Lamenting his Untimely Death,
When Henry, with his Latest Breath,
Cried –

"Oh, my Friends, be warned by me,

That Breakfast, Dinner, Lunch and Tea
Are all the Human Frame requires ..."
With that the Wretched Child expires.

Matilda,

Who told Lies, and was Burned to Death.

Matilda told such Dreadful Lies,

It made one Gasp and Stretch one's Eyes;
Her Aunt, who, from her Earliest Youth,
Had kept a Strict Regard for Truth,

Attempted to Believe Matilda:
The effort very nearly killed her,
And would have done so, had not She
Discovered this Infirmity.
For once, towards the Close of Day,
Matilda, growing tired of play,

And finding she was left alone,
Went tiptoe

to

the Telephone
And summoned the Immediate Aid
Of London's Noble Fire-Brigade.
Within an hour the Gallant Band
Were pouring in on every hand,
From Putney, Hackney Downs and Bow,
With Courage high and Hearts a-glow
They galloped, roaring through the Town,

"Matilda's House is Burning Down!"
Inspired by British Cheers and Loud
Proceeding from the Frenzied Crowd,
They ran their ladders through a score
Of windows on the Ball Room Floor;
And took Peculiar Pains to Souse
The Pictures up and down the House,

Until Matilda's Aunt succeeded
In showing them they were not needed
And even then she had to pay
To get the Men to go away!

* * *

It happened that a few Weeks later
Her Aunt was off to the Theatre
To see that Interesting Play

The Second Mrs. Tanqueray.

She had refused to take her Niece
To hear this Entertaining Piece:
A Deprivation Just and Wise
To Punish her for Telling Lies.
That Night a Fire *did* break out –
You should have heard Matilda Shout!
You should have heard her Scream and Bawl,

And throw the window up and call
To People passing in the Street –
(The rapidly increasing Heat
Encouraging her to obtain
Their confidence) – but all in vain!
For every time She shouted "Fire!"

They only answered "Little Liar!"
And therefore when her Aunt returned,

Matilda, and the House, were Burned.

Franklin Hyde,

Who caroused in the Dirt and was corrected by His Uncle.

His Uncle came on Franklin Hyde
Carousing in the Dirt.
He Shook him hard from Side to Side
And

Hit him till it Hurt,

Exclaiming, with a Final Thud,

"Take

that! Abandoned Boy!
For Playing with Disgusting Mud
As though it were a Toy!"

MORAL

From Franklin Hyde's adventure, learn
To pass your Leisure Time

In Cleanly Merriment, and turn
From Mud and Ooze and Slime
And every form of Nastiness –
But, on the other Hand,
Children in ordinary Dress
May always play with Sand.

Godolphin Horne,

Who was cursed with the Sin of Pride, and Became a Boot-Black.

Godolphin Horne was Nobly Born;
He held the Human Race in Scorn,
And lived with all his Sisters where
His father lived, in Berkeley Square.
And oh! the Lad was Deathly Proud!

He never shook your Hand or Bowed,
But merely smirked and nodded

thus:

How perfectly ridiculous!
Alas! That such Affected Tricks
Should flourish in a Child of Six!
(For such was Young Godolphin's age).

Just then, the Court required a Page,
Whereat

the Lord High Chamberlain
(The Kindest and the Best of Men),
He went good-naturedly and

took
A Perfectly Enormous Book
Called *People Qualified to Be*
Attendant on His Majesty,
And murmured, as he scanned the list
(To see that no one should be missed),
"There's

William Coutts has got the
Flue,

And Billy Higgs would never do,

And Guy  de Vere is far too young,

And ... wasn't D'Alton's Father hung?
And as for Alexander Byng! – ...
I think I know the kind of thing,
A Churchman, cleanly, nobly born,
Come

let us say Godolphin Horne?"
But hardly had he said a word
When Murmurs of Dissent were heard.
The King of Iceland's Eldest Son
Said, "Thank you! I am taking none!"
The Aged Duchess of Athlone
Remarked, in her sub-acid tone,
"I doubt if He is what we need!"
With which the Bishops all agreed;
And even Lady Mary Flood
(*So* Kind, and oh! so *really* good)
Said, "No! He wouldn't do at all,
He'd make us feel a lot too small."
The Chamberlain said,

" . . . Well, well, well!
No doubt you're right. . . . One cannot tell!"
He took his Gold and Diamond Pen
And

   Scratched Godolphin out again.
So now Godolphin is the Boy

Who blacks the Boots at the Savoy.

Algernon,

*Who played with a Loaded Gun, and, on missing his
Sister was reprimanded by his Father.*

Young Algernon, the Doctor's
    Son,
Was

    playing with a
    Loaded Gun.
He pointed it to-
    wards his sister,
Aimed very care-
    fully, but

Missed her!

His Father, who was standing near

The Loud Explosion chanced to Hear,

And reprimanded Algernon
For playing with a Loaded Gun.

Hildebrand,

Who was frightened by a Passing Motor, and was brought to Reason.

"Oh, Murder! What was that, Papa!"
"My child,

It was a Motor-Car,
A Most Ingenious Toy!

Designed to Captivate and Charm
Much rather than to rouse Alarm
In any English Boy.

"What would your Great Grandfather who

Was Aide-de-Camp to General Brue,

And lost a leg at

Waterloo,

And

Quatre-Bras and

Ligny too!

And died at Trafalgar! –

What would he have remarked to hear
His Young Descendant shriek with fear,
Because he happened to be near
    A Harmless Motor-Car!
But do not fret about it! Come!

We'll off to Town

And purchase some!"

Lord Lundy,

Who was too Freely Moved to Tears, and thereby ruined his Political Career.

Lord Lundy from his earliest years
Was far too freely moved to Tears.
For instance if his Mother said,
"Lundy! It's time to go to Bed!"
He bellowed like a Little Turk.
Or if

his father Lord Dunquerque
Said "Hi!" in a Commanding Tone,
"Hi, Lundy! Leave the Cat alone!"
Lord Lundy, letting go its tail,
Would raise so terrible a wail
As moved

His

    Grandpapa

        the

        Duke

To utter the severe rebuke:
"When I, Sir! was a little Boy,
An Animal was not a Toy!"

His father's Elder Sister, who
Was married to a Parvenoo,

Confided to Her Husband, "Drat!
The Miserable, Peevish Brat!
Why don't they drown the Little Beast?"
Suggestions which, to say the least,
Are not what we expect to hear
From Daughters of an English Peer.
His grandmamma, His Mother's Mother,

Who had some dignity or other,
The Garter, or no matter what,
I can't remember all the Lot!
Said "Oh! that I were Brisk and Spry
To give him that for which to cry!"
(An empty wish, alas! for she

Was Blind and nearly ninety-three).

The

Dear old Butler

          thought – but there!
I really neither know nor care
For what the Dear Old Butler thought!
In my opinion, Butlers ought
To know their place, and not to play
The Old Retainer night and day

I'm getting tired and so are you,
Let's cut the Poem into two!

* * *

Lord Lundy

(SECOND CANTO)

It happened to Lord Lundy then,
As happens to so many men:
Towards the age of twenty-six,
They shoved him into politics;
In which profession he commanded
The income that his rank demanded
In turn as Secretary for
India, the Colonies, and War.
But very soon his friends began
To doubt if he were quite the man:
Thus, if a member rose to say
(As members do from day to day),

"Arising out of that reply . . . !"

Lord Lundy would begin to cry.
A Hint at harmless little jobs
Would shake him with convulsive sobs.

While as for Revelations, these
Would simply bring him to his knees,
And leave him whimpering like a child.
It drove his Colleagues raving wild!
They let him sink from Post to Post,
From fifteen hundred at the most
To eight, and barely six – and then
To be Curator of Big Ben! . . .
And finally there came a Threat
To oust him from the Cabinet!

The Duke – his aged grand-sire – bore
The shame till he could bear no more.
He rallied his declining powers,
Summoned the youth to Brackley Towers,

And bitterly addressed him thus –
"Sir! you have disappointed us!
We had intended you to be
The next Prime Minister but three:
The stocks were sold; the Press was squared:
The Middle Class was quite prepared.
But as it is! . . . My language fails!

Go out and govern New South Wales!"

* * *

The Aged Patriot groaned and died:

And gracious! how Lord Lundy cried!

Rebecca,

Who slammed Doors for Fun and Perished Miserably.

A Trick that everyone abhors
In Little Girls is slamming Doors.
A

Wealthy Banker's

Little Daughter

Who lived in Palace Green, Bayswater
(By name Rebecca Offendort),
Was given to this Furious Sport.

She would deliberately go

And Slam the door like
          Billy-Ho!

To make

her

Uncle Jacob start.
She was not really bad at heart,
But only rather rude and wild:
She was an aggravating child....

It happened that a Marble Bust
Of Abraham was standing just
Above the Door this little Lamb
Had carefully prepared to Slam,
And Down it came! It knocked her flat!

It laid her out! She looked
like that.

* * *

Her funeral Sermon (which was long
And followed by a Sacred Song)
Mentioned her Virtues, it is true,
But dwelt upon her Vices too,

And showed the Dreadful End of One
Who goes and slams the door for Fun.

* * *

The children who were brought to hear
The awful Tale from far and near
Were much impressed,

and inly swore

They never more would slam the Door.

– As often they had done before.

George,

Who played with a Dangerous Toy, and suffered a Catastrophe of considerable Dimensions.

When George's Grandmamma was told

That George had been as good as Gold,
She Promised in the Afternoon
To buy him an *Immense BALLOON.*
        And

so she did; but when it came,
It got into the candle flame,
And being of a dangerous sort
Exploded

with a loud report!

The Lights went out! The Windows broke!
The Room was filled with reeking smoke.
And in the darkness shrieks and yells
Were mingled with Electric Bells,
And falling masonry and groans,
And crunching, as of broken bones,
And dreadful shrieks, when, worst of all,
The House itself began to fall!
It tottered, shuddered to and fro,
Then crashed into the street below –
Which happened to be Savile Row.

       *   *   *

When Help arrived, among the Dead

Were  Cousin Mary,

Little Fred,

The Footmen

(both of them),

The Groom,

The man that cleaned the Billiard-Room,

The Chaplain, and

The Still-Room Maid.
And I am dreadfully afraid
That Monsieur Champignon, the Chef,
Will now be

permanently deaf –
And both his

Aides  are much the same;
While George, who was in part to blame,
Received, you will regret to hear,
A nasty lump

behind the ear.

MORAL

The moral is that little Boys
Should not be given dangerous Toys.

Charles Augustus Fortescue,

Who always Did what was Right, and so accumulated an Immense Fortune.

The nicest child I ever knew
Was Charles Augustus Fortescue.
He never lost his cap, or tore
His stockings or his pinafore:
   In eating Bread he made no Crumbs,
   He was extremely fond
     of sums,

To which, however, he
   preferred
The Parsing of a Latin
   Word –
He sought, when it was in
   his power,
For information twice an hour,

And as for finding Mutton-Fat
Unappetising, far from that!
He often, at his Father's Board,
Would beg them, of his own accord,

To give him, if they did not mind,
The Greasiest Morsels they could find –
His Later Years did not belie
The Promise of his Infancy.

In Public Life he always tried
To take a judgment Broad and Wide;

In Private, none was more than he
Renowed for quiet courtesy.
He rose at once in his Career,
And long before his Fortieth Year
Had wedded

Fifi,

Only Child
Of Bunyan, First Lord Aberfylde.
He thus became immensely Rich,
And built the Splendid Mansion which
Is called

"The Cedars, Muswell Hill,"

Where he resides in Affluence still,
To show what Everybody might
Become by

SIMPLY DOING RIGHT.

ILLUSTRATED BY NICOLAS BENTLEY

NEW CAUTIONARY TALES

A Reproof of Gluttony

The Elephant will eat of hay
Some four and twenty tons a day,

And in his little eyes express
His unaffected thankfulness

That Providence should deign to find
Him food of this delicious kind.

While they that pay for all the hay
Will frequently be heard to say
How highly privileged they feel
To help him make so large a meal.

The Boa Constrictor

dotes on goats;

The Horse is quite content with oats,
Or will alternatively pass
A happy morning munching grass.

The great Ant Eater of Taluz

Consumes – or people say he does –
Not only what his name implies
But even ordinary flies:
And Marmosets and Chimpanzees
Are happy on the nuts of trees.

The Lion from the burning slopes
Of Atlas lives on Antelopes,
And only adds the flesh of men

By way of relish now and then;
As Cheetahs – yes, and Tigers, too,
And Jaguars of the Andes – do.

The Lobster, I have heard it said,
Eats nobody till he is dead;
And Cobras, though they have the sense
      To poison you in self-defence,

Restrict their food to birds and hares:
Which also may be true of Bears.

Indeed wherever we survey
Our Humble Friends we find that they
Confine their appetites to what
May happen to be on the spot.
Simplicity and moderation
Distinguish all the Brute Creation.
But Man – proud man! (as Dryden sings)
Though wolfing quantities of things –
Smoked Salmon in transparent slices,
And Turbot à la Reine,

and Ices,

And Truffled Pies

and Caviare,

And Chinese Ginger

from the Jar;

And Oysters; and a kind of stuff
Called Cassouletto (good enough!)
And Mutton duly steeped in claret
(Or jumped with young shallot and carrot),
And Chicken Livers done with rice,
And Quails (which, I am told are Mice),
And Peaches from a sunny wall,
And – Lord! I don't know what and all! –

Oh! Yes! And Sausages

– is not

Contented with his Prandial lot.

MORAL

The Moral is (I think, at least)
That Man is an UNGRATEFUL BEAST.

Maria

Who made Faces and a Deplorable Marriage

Maria loved to pull a face:

And no such commonplace grimace
As you or I or anyone
Might make at grandmamma for fun.

But one where nose and mouth and all
Were screwed into a kind of ball,

The which – as you may well expect –
Produced a horrible effect
On those it was directed at.

One morning she was struck like that! –
Her features took their final mould
In shapes that made your blood run cold
And wholly lost their former charm.

Mamma, in agonised alarm,
Consulted a renowned Masseuse
– An old and valued friend of hers –

Who rubbed the wretched child for days
In five and twenty different ways
And after that began again.
But all in vain! – But all in vain!

The years advance: Maria grows
Into a Blooming English Rose –
With every talent, every grace
(Save in this trifle of the face).
She sang, recited, laughed and played
At all that an accomplished maid
Should play with skill to be of note –
Golf, the Piano, and the Goat;
She talked in French till all was blue
And knew a little German too.

She told the tales that soldiers tell,

She also danced extremely well,
Her wit was pointed, loud and raw,
She shone at laying down the law,
She drank liqueurs instead of tea,

Her verse was admirably free
And quoted in the latest books –
But people couldn't stand her looks.

Her parents had with thoughtful care
Proclaimed her genius everywhere,

Nor quite concealed a wealth which sounds
Enormous – thirty million pounds –

And

further whispered it that she
Could deal with it exclusively.

They did not hide her chief defect,
But what with birth and intellect
And breeding and such ample means,
And still in her delightful 'teens,
A girl like our Maria (they thought)
Should make the kind of match she ought.
Those who had seen her here at home
Might hesitate: but Paris? Rome?. . .
– The foreigners should take the bait.

And so they did. At any rate,
The greatest men of every land

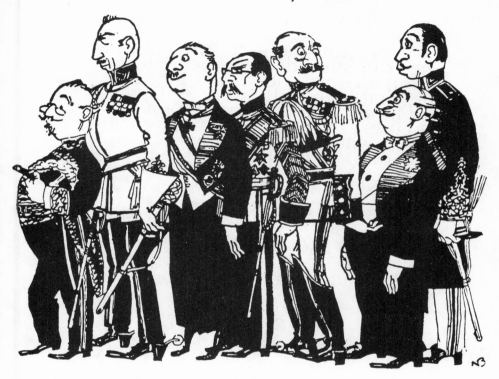

Arrived in shoals to seek her hand,
Grand Dukes, Commanders of the Fleece,
Mysterious Millionaires from Greece,
And exiled Kings in large amounts,

Ambassadors and Papal Counts,
And Rastaqouères from Palamerez
And Famous Foreign Secretairies,
They came along in turns to call
But *all* – without exception, *all* –
Though with determination set,
Yet, when they actually *met*,

Would start
    convulsively
        as though

They had received a sudden blow,

And mumbling a discreet good-day

Would shuffle, turn and slink away.

The upshot of it was Maria
Was married to a neighbouring Squire
Who, being blind, could never guess
His wife's appalling ugliness.

The man was independent, dull,
Offensive, poor and masterful.
It was a very dreadful thing! . . .
Now let us turn to Sarah Byng.

Sarah Byng

Who could not read and was tossed into a thorny hedge by a Bull

Some years ago you heard me sing
My doubts on Alexander Byng.
His sister Sarah now inspires
My jaded Muse, my failing fires.
Of Sarah Byng the tale is told
How when the child was twelve years old
She could not read or write a line.

Her sister Jane, though barely nine,
Could spout the Catechism through

And parts of Matthew Arnold too,

While little Bill
  who came between

Was quite unnaturally keen
   On
      "Athalie," by Jean Racine.

But not so Sarah! Not so Sal!

She was a most uncultured girl
Who didn't care a pinch of snuff
For any literary stuff

And gave the classics all a miss.
Observe the consequence of this!
As she was walking home one day,
Upon the fields across her way
A gate, securely padlocked, stood,
And by its side a piece of wood
On which was painted plain and full,

BE WARE
THE VERY
FURIOUS
BULL

BEWARE THE VERY FURIOUS BULL.

Alas!
   The young illiterate
Went blindly forward to
   her fate,
And ignorantly climbed
   the gate!

Now happily the Bull that day
Was rather in the mood for play
Than goring people through and through
As Bulls so very often do:

He tossed her lightly with his horns
Into a prickly hedge of thorns,
And stood by laughing while she strode
And pushed and struggled to the road.

The lesson was not lost upon
The child, who since has always gone
A long way round to keep away
From signs, whatever they may say,
And leaves a padlocked gate alone.
Moreover she has wisely grown
Confirmed in her instinctive guess

That literature breeds distress.

Jack and his Pony, Tom

Jack had a little pony – Tom;

He frequently would take it from
The stable where it used to stand
And give it sugar with his hand.

He also gave it oats and hay
And carrots twenty times a day
And grass in basketfuls, and greens,
And swedes and mangolds also beans
And patent foods from various sources
And bread (which isn't good for horses)
And chocolate and apple-rings
And lots and lots of other things
The most of which do not agree
With Polo Ponies such as he.
And all in such a quantity
As ruined his digestion wholly
And turned him from a Ponopoly
– I mean a Polo Pony – into
A case that clearly must be seen to.

Because he swelled and swelled and swelled.
Which, when the kindly boy beheld,

He gave him medicine by the pail
And malted milk, and nutmeg ale,
And yet it only swelled the more
Until its stomach touched the floor,

And then it heaved and groaned as well
And staggered, till at last it fell
And found it could not rise again.
Jack wept and prayed – but all in vain.

The pony died and as it died
Kicked him severely in the side.

MORAL

Kindness to animals should be
Attuned to their brutality.

Tom and his Pony, Jack

Tom had a little pony, Jack:

He vaulted lightly on its back
And galloped off for miles and miles,
A-leaping hedges, gates and stiles,

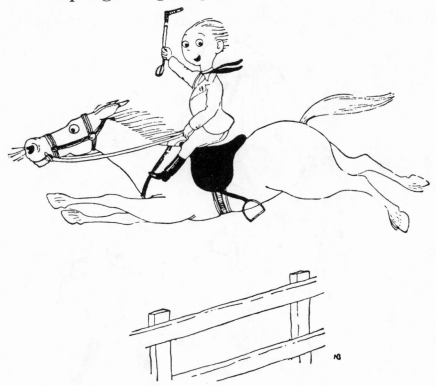

And shouting "Yoicks!" and "Tally-Ho!"
And "Heads I win!" and "Tails below!"

And many another sporting phrase.
He rode like this for several days,
Until the pony, feeling tired,
Collapsed, looked heavenward and expired.

His father made a fearful row.
He said "By Gum, you've done it now!
Here lies – a carcase on the ground –
No less than five and twenty pound!

Indeed the value of the beast
Would probably have much increased.
His teeth were false; and all were told

That he was only four
    years old.
Oh! Curse it all! I tell you plain
I'll never let you ride again."

MORAL

His father died when he was twenty
And left three horses, which is plenty.

About John,

Who lost a Fortune by Throwing Stones

JOHN VAVASSOUR
DE QUENTIN JONES

Was very fond
of throwing
stones

At Horses, People, Passing Trains,
But 'specially at Window-panes.

Like many of the Upper Class

He liked the Sound of Broken Glass*

*A line I stole with subtle daring
From Wing-Com-
mander Maurice Baring

It bucked him up and made him gay:
It was his favourite form of Play.
But the Amusement cost him dear,
My children, as you now shall hear.

JOHN VAVASSOUR DE QUENTIN had
An uncle, who adored the lad:

And often chuckled; "Wait until
You see what's left you in my will!"

Nor were the words without import,
Because this uncle did a sort
Of something in the City, which
Had made him fabulously rich.
(Although his brother, John's papa,
Was poor, as many fathers are.)

He had a lot of stocks and shares
And half a street in Buenos Aires*
A bank in Rio, and a line
Of Steamers to the Argentine.
And options more than I can tell,
And bits of Canada as well;
He even had a mortgage on
The House inhabited by John.
His will, the cause of all the fuss,
Was carefully indited thus:

"This is the last and solemn Will
Of Uncle William – known as Bill.

*But this pronunciation varies.
Some people call it Bu-enos Airés.

I do bequeath, devise and give
By Execution Mandative
The whole amount of what I've got
(It comes to a tremendous lot!)
In seizin to devolve upon
      My well-beloved nephew John.

(And here the witnesses will sign
Their names upon the dotted line.)"

Such was the Legal Instrument
Expressing Uncle Bill's intent.

As time went on declining Health
Transmogrified this Man of Wealth;
And it was excellently clear
That Uncle Bill's demise was near.

At last his sole idea of fun
Was sitting snoozling in the
sun

So once, when he would
take the air,
They wheeled him in his
Patent Chair

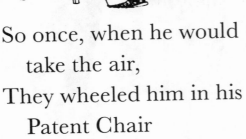

(By "They," I mean his Nurse, who came
From Dorchester upon the Thame:
Miss Charming was the Nurse's name).
To where beside a little wood
A long abandoned green-house stood,
And there he sank into a doze
Of senile and inept repose.
But not for long his drowsy ease!
A stone came whizzing through the trees,
And caught him smartly in the eye.
He woke with an appalling cry,
And shrieked in agonizing tones:
"Oh! Lord! Whoever's throwing stones!"

Miss Charming, who was standing near,
Said: "That was Master John, I fear!"

"Go, get my Ink-pot and my Quill,
My Blotter and my Famous Will."

Miss Charming flew as
though on wings

To fetch these necessary
things,

And Uncle William ran his pen
Through "well-beloved John," and then
Proceeded, in the place of same,
To substitute Miss Charming's name:

Who now resides in Portman Square
And is accepted everywhere.

Peter Goole

Who Ruined his Father and Mother by Extravagance

PART I

Young Peter Goole, a child of
  nine
Gave little reason to complain.
Though an imaginative youth
He very often told the truth,
And never tried to black the eyes
Of Comrades of superior size.

He did his lessons (more or less)
Without extravagant distress,
And showed sufficient intellect,
But failed in one severe defect;
It seems he wholly lacked a sense
Of limiting the day's expense,
And money ran between his hands
Like water through the Ocean Sands.
Such conduct could not but affect
His parent's fortune, which was wrecked
Like many and many another one
By folly in a spendthrift son:
By that most tragical mischance,
An Only Child's Extravagance.

There came a day when Mr. Goole
– The Father of this little fool –
With nothing in the bank at all
Was up against it, like a wall.

He wrang his hands, exclaiming, "If

I only I had a bit of Stiff
How different would be my life!"
Whereat his true and noble wife

Replied, to comfort him, "Alas!
I said that this would come to pass!
Nothing can keep us off the rocks
But Peter's little Money Box."
The Father, therefore (and his wife),

They prised it open with a knife –

But nothing could be found therein
Save two bone buttons and a pin.

PART II

They had to sell the house and grounds

For less than twenty thousand pounds,

And so retired,

with broken hearts,

To vegetate in foreign parts,

And ended their declining years
At Blidah – which is near Algiers.
There in the course of time
      they died,

   And there lie buried
     side by side.

While when we turn to Peter, he
The cause of this catastrophe,
There fell upon him such a fate
As makes me shudder to relate.
Just in its fifth and final year,
His University Career
Was blasted by the new and dread
Necessity of earning bread.
He was compelled to join a firm
Of Brokers – in the summer term!

And even now, at twenty-five,

He has to
W O R K
    to
keep alive!

Yes! All day long from 10 till 4!
For half the year or even more;

With but an hour or two to spend
At luncheon with a city friend.

Aunt Jane

"Mamma" said AMANDA "I want to know what
   Our relatives mean when they say
That Aunt Jane is a Gorgon who ought to be shot,
   Or at any rate taken away.

"Pray what is a Gorgon and why do you shoot

It? Or are its advances refused?
Or is it perhaps a maleficent Brute?
    I protest I am wholly bemused."

"The Term," said her Mother, "is certain to pain,
    And is quite inexcusably rude.
Moveover Aunt Jane, though uncommonly plain,
    Is also uncommonly good.

"She provides information without hesitation,
    For people unwilling to learn;

And often bestows good advice

upon those

Who give her no thanks in return.

"She is down before anyone's up in the place –
  That is, up before anyone's down.

Her Domestics are awed by the shape of her face
And they tremble with fear at her frown.

"Her visiting list is of Clergymen who
Have reached a respectable age,

And she pays her companion
MISS ANGELA DREW
A sufficient and regular wage.

"Her fortune is large, though we often remark
    On a modesty rare in the rich;
For her nearest and dearest are quite in the dark
    As to what she will leave, or to which.

"Her conduct has ever been totally free
    From censorious whispers of ill,
At any rate, since 1903 –
    And probably earlier still.

"Your Father's dear sister presents in a word,
    A model for all of her sex,
With a firmness of will that is never deterred,
    And a confidence nothing can vex.

"I can only desire that you too should aspire
    To such earthly reward as appears
In a high reputation, at present entire,
    After Heaven knows how many years.

"So in future remember to turn a deaf ear
  To detraction – and now run away
To your brothers and sisters whose laughter I hear
  In the garden below us at play."
"Oh, thank you, Mamma!" said AMANDA at
  that,

And ran off to

the innocent band
Who were merrily burying Thomas the Cat
Right up to his neck in the sand.

On Food

Alas! What various tastes in food,
Divide the human brotherhood!

Birds in their little nests agree

With Chinamen,

but

not with me.

Colonials like their oysters hot,
Their omelettes heavy – I do not.

The French are
fond of slugs
and frogs,

The Siamese eat
puppy-dogs.

The nobles at the brilliant Court
Of Muscovy, consumed a sort
Of candles held and eaten

thus

As though they were asparagus.

The Spaniard, I have heard it said,
Eats garlic, by itself, on bread:
Now just suppose a friend or dun
Dropped in to lunch at half-past one
And you were jovially to say,

"Here's bread and garlic! Peg away!"
I doubt if you would gain your end
Or soothe the dun, or please the friend.

In Italy the traveller notes
With great disgust the flesh of goats
Appearing on the table d'hôtes;

And even this the natives spoil
By frying it in rancid oil.

In Maryland they charge like sin
For nasty stuff called terrapin;
And when they ask you out to dine
At Washington, instead of wine,

They give you water from the spring
With lumps of ice for flavouring,
That sometimes kill and always freeze
The high plenipotentiaries.

In Massachusetts all the way
From Boston down to Buzzards Bay
They feed you till you want to die
On rhubarb pie and pumpkin pie,
And horrible huckleberry pie,
And when you summon the strength to cry,
"What is there else that I can try?"
They stare at you in mild surprise
And serve you other kinds of pies.
And I with these mine eyes have seen
A dreadful stuff called Margarine
Consumed by men in Bethnal Green.
But I myself that here complain
Confess restriction quite in vain.
I feel my native courage fail
To see a Gascon eat a snail;
I dare not ask abroad for tea;

No cannibal can dine with me;
And all the world is torn and rent
By varying views on nutriment.
And yet upon the other hand,
De gustibus non disputand —
                              — *Um.*

THE BAD CHILD'S
BOOK OF BEASTS

DEDICATION

To
Master EVELYN BELL
Of Oxford

Evelyn Bell,
I love you well.

INTRODUCTION

I CALL you bad, my little child,
    Upon the title page,
Because a manner rude and wild
    Is common at your age.

The Moral of this priceless work
    (If rightly understood)
Will make you – from a little Turk –
    Unnaturally good.

Do not as evil children do,
  Who on the slightest grounds
Will imitate

  the Kangaroo,
With wild unmeaning bounds:

Do not as children badly bred,
　　Who eat like little Hogs,
And when they have to go to bed
　　Will whine like Puppy Dogs:

Who take their manners from the Ape,
　　Their habits from the Bear,
Indulge the loud unseemly jape,
　　And never brush their hair.

But so control your actions that
   Your friends may all repeat.

"This child is dainty as the Cat,
   And as the Owl discreet."

The Yak

As a friend to the children

commend me the Yak.

You will find it exactly the thing:
It will carry and fetch,

you can ride on its back,

Or lead it about

with a string.

The Tartar who dwells on the plains of Thibet
(A desolate region of snow)

Has for centuries made it a nursery pet,
And surely the Tartar should know!

Then tell your papa where the Yak can be got,

And if he is awfully rich
He will buy you the creature –

or else

he will *not.*

(I cannot be positive which.)

The Polar Bear

The Polar Bear is unaware

Of cold that cuts me through:
For why? He has a coat of hair.
I wish I had one too!

The Lion

The Lion, the Lion, he dwells in the waste,
He has a big head and a very small waist;

But his shoulders are stark, and his jaws they are
grim,
And a good little child will not play with him.

The Tiger

The Tiger on the other hand,

is kittenish and mild,
He makes a pretty playfellow for any little child;
And mothers of large families (who claim to com-
mon sense)

Will find a Tiger well repay the trouble and
expense.

The Dromedary

The Dromedary is a cheerful bird:

I cannot say the same about the Kurd.

The Whale

The Whale that wanders round the Pole

Is not

a table fish.
You cannot bake or boil him whole
Nor serve him in a dish;

But you may cut his blubber up
And melt it down for oil.

And so replace

the colza bean
(A product of the soil).

These facts should all be noted down
And ruminated on,

By every boy in Oxford town
Who wants to be a Don.

The Camel

"The Ship of the Desert"

The Hippopotamus

I shoot the Hippopotamus

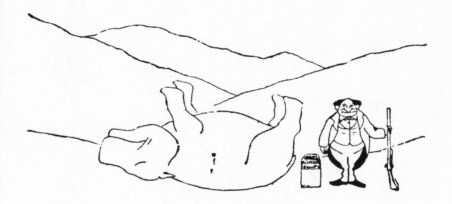

with bullets made of platinum,

Because if I use leaden ones

his hide is sure to flatten 'em.

The Dodo

The Dodo used

to walk around,

And take the sun and air.
The sun yet warms his native ground —

The Dodo is not there!

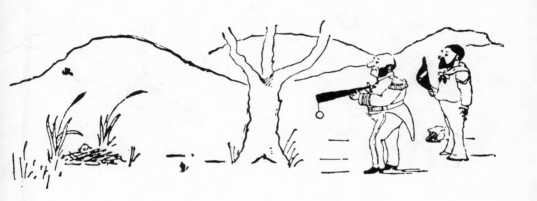

The voice which used to squawk and squeak
Is now for ever dumb –

Yet may you see his bones and beak
All in the Mu-se-um.

The Marmozet

The species Man and Marmozet
Are intimately linked;

The Marmozet survives as yet,
But Men are all extinct.

The Camelopard

The Camelopard it is said
    By travellers (who never lie),

He cannot stretch out straight in bed
Because he is so high.
The clouds surround his lofty head,
His hornlets touch the sky.

How shall
I hunt
I
this quadruped?
cannot tell!
Not I!

(A picture of how people try
And fail to hit that head so high.)

I'll buy a little parachute
(A common parachute with wings),
I'll fill it full of arrowroot
And other necessary things,

And I will slay this fearful brute
With stones and sticks and guns and slings.

(A picture of

how people shoot
With comfort from a parachute.)

The Learned Fish

This learned Fish has not sufficient brains
To go into the water when it rains.

The Elephant

When people call this beast to mind,

They marvel more and more
At such a

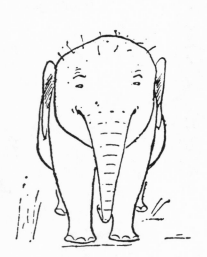

LITTLE tail behind,

So *LARGE* a trunk before.

The Big Baboon

The Big Baboon is found upon
The plains of Cariboo:

He goes about

with nothing on
(A shocking thing to do).

But if he

dressed respectably
And let his whiskers grow,

How like this Big Baboon would be

To Mister So-and so!

The Rhinoceros

Rhinoceros, your hide looks all undone,

You do not take my fancy in the least:

You have a horn where other brutes have none:
    Rhinoceros, you are an ugly beast.

The Frog

Be kind and tender to the Frog,

And do not call him names,
As 'Slimy skin,' or 'Polly-wog'
  Or likewise 'Ugly James,'
Or 'Gap-a-grin,' or 'Toad-gone-wrong,'
  Or 'Bill Bandy-knees':

The Frog is justly sensitive
  To epithets like these.

No animal will more repay
  A treatment kind and fair;
At least

  so lonely people say
Who keep a frog (and, by the way,
They are extremely rare).

Oh! My!

MORE BEASTS
FOR WORSE
CHILDREN

DEDICATION

To

Miss ALICE WOLCOTT BRINLEY,

of Philadelphia

MORE BEASTS

FOR WORSE CHILDREN

INTRODUCTION

The parents of the learned child
    (His father and his mother)
Were utterly aghast to note
The facts he would at random quote
On creatures curious, rare and wild;
    And wondering, asked each other:

"An idle little child like this,
　　How is it that he knows
What years of close analysis
　　Are powerful to disclose?

Our brains are trained, our books are big
　　And yet we always fail

To answer why the Guinea-pig
Is born without a tail.

Or why the Wanderoo* should rant
In wild, unmeaning rhymes,

*Sometimes called the "Lion-tailed or tufted Baboon of Ceylon."

Whereas the Indian Elephant
Will only read *The Times*.

Perhaps he found a way to slip
 Unnoticed to the Zoo,
And gave the Pachyderm a tip,
 Or pumped the Wanderoo.

Or even by an artful plan
 Deceived our watchful eyes,
And interviewed the Pelican,
 Who is extremely wise."

"Oh! no," said he, in humble tone,
   With shy but conscious look,
"Such facts I never could have known
   But for this little book."

The Python

A PYTHON I should not advise, –
It needs a doctor for its eyes,
And has the measles yearly.

However, if you feel inclined
To get one (to improve your mind,
And not from fashion merely),
Allow no music near its cage;

And when it flies into a rage
Chastise it, most severely.

I had an aunt in Yucatan
Who bought a Python from a man
  And kept it for a pet.
She died, because she never knew
These simple little rules and few; —

The Snake is living yet.

The Welsh Mutton

The Cambrian Welsh or Mountain Sheep
    Is of the Ovine race,
His conversation is not deep,
    But then – observe his face!

The Porcupine

What! would you slap the Porcupine?
Unhappy child – desist!
Alas! that any friend of mine
Should turn Tupto-philist.*

* From τυπτω = I strike; φιλέω = I love; one that loves to strike. The word is not found in classical Greek, nor does it occur among the writers of the Renaissance – nor anywhere else.

To strike the meanest and the least
Of creatures is a sin,

How much more bad to beat a beast
With prickles on its skin.

The Scorpion

The Scorpion is as black as soot,
    He dearly loves to bite;
He is a most unpleasant brute
    To find in bed, at night.

The Crocodile

Whatever our faults, we can always engage
That no fancy or fable shall sully our page,
So take note of what follows, I beg.
This creature so grand and august in its age,
In its youth is hatched out of an egg.

And oft in some far Coptic town
The Missionary sits him down
   To breakfast by the Nile:
The heart beneath his priestly gown
   Is innocent of guile;

When suddenly the rigid frown
Of Panic is observed to drown
His customary smile.

Why does he start and leap amain,

And scour the sandy Libyan plain

Like one that wants to catch a train,

Or wrestles with internal pain?

Because he finds his egg contain –
Green, hungry, horrible and plain –
An Infant Crocodile.

The Vulture

The Vulture eats between his meals,
  And that's the reason why

He very, very rarely feels
　　As well as you and I.

His eye is dull, his head is bald,
　　His neck is growing thinner.
Oh! what a lesson for us all
　　To only eat at dinner!

The Bison

The Bison is vain, and (I write it with pain)
The Door-mat you see on his head

Is not, as some learned professors maintain,
The opulent growth of a genius' brain;

But is sewn on with needle and thread.

The Viper

Yet another great truth I record in my verse,

That some Vipers are venomous, some the reverse;

    A fact you may prove if you try,

By procuring two Vipers, and letting them bite;

With the *first* you are only the worse for a fright,

But after the *second* you die.

The Llama

The Llama is a woolly sort of fleecy hairy goat,
With an indolent expression and an undulating thro:
Like an unsuccessful literary man.

And I know the place he lives in (or at least –
I think I do)
It is Ecuador, Brazil or Chile – possibly Peru;
You must find it in the Atlas if you can.

The Llama of the Pampasses you never should
confound
(In spite of a deceptive similarity of sound)
   With the Lhama who is Lord of Turkestan.

or the former is a beautiful and valuable beast,
But the latter is not lovable nor useful in the least;
And the Ruminant is preferable surely to the Priest
Who battens on the woeful superstitions of the East,
    The Mongol of the Monastery of Shan.

The Chamois

The Chamois inhabits
Lucerne, where his habits
    (Though why I have not an idea-r)
Give him sudden short spasms
On the brink of deep chasms,
    And he lives in perpetual fear.

The Frozen Mammoth

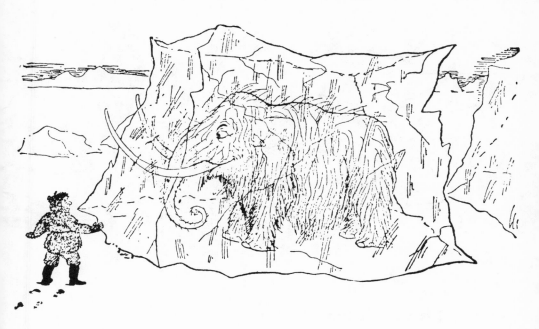

This Creature, though rare, is still found to the East
Of the Northern Siberian Zone.

It is known to the whole of that primitive group
That the carcase will furnish an excellent soup,
  Though the cooking it offers one drawback at lea
  (Of a serious nature I own):

If the skin be *but punctured* before it is boiled,
Your confection is wholly and utterly spoiled.

And hence (on account of the size of the beast)
The dainty is nearly unknown.

The Microbe

The Microbe is so very small
You cannot make him out at all,
But many sanguine people hope
To see him through a microscope.
His jointed tongue that lies beneath
A hundred curious rows of teeth;
His seven tufted tails with lots
Of lovely pink and purple spots,

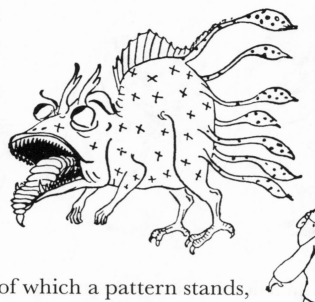

On each of which a pattern stands,
Composed of forty separate bands;
His eyebrows of a tender green;
All these have never yet been seen –
But Scientists, who ought to know,
Assure us that they must be so. . . .
Oh! let us never, never doubt
What nobody is sure about!

MORE PEERS

Verses by H. BELLOC
Pictures by B. T. B.

Lord Roehampton

During a late election Lord
Roehampton strained a vocal chord
From shouting, very loud and high,
To lots and lots of people why
The Budget in his own opin-
-Ion should not be allowed to win.

He

sought a Specialist, who said:
"You have a swelling in the head:
Your Larynx is a thought relaxed
And you are greatly over-taxed."

"I am indeed! On every side!"
The Earl (for such he was) replied

In hoarse excitement. . . . "Oh! My Lord,
You jeopardize your vocal chord!"
Broke in the worthy Specialist.
"Come! Here's the treatment! I insist!
To Bed! to Bed! And do not speak
A single word till Wednesday week,
When I will come and set you free
(If you are cured) and take my fee."

On Wednesday week the Doctor hires
A Brand-new Car with Brand-new Tyres
And Brand-new Chauffeur all complete
For visiting South Audley Street.

* * *

But what is this? No Union Jack
Floats on the Stables at the back!
No Toffs escorting Ladies fair
Perambulate the Gay Parterre.
A 'Scutcheon hanging lozenge-wise
And draped in crape appals his eyes
Upon the mansion's ample door,
To which he wades through

heaps of Straw,[†]

[†] This is the first and only time
That I have used this sort of Rhyme.

And which a Butler, drowned in tears,
On opening but confirms his fears:
"Oh! Sir! – Prepare to hear the worst! ...
Last night my kind old master burst.
And what is more, I doubt if he
Has left enough to pay your fee.
The Budget –"

With a dreadful oath,

The Specialist,

denouncing both
The Budget *and* the House of Lords,
Buzzed angrily Bayswaterwards.

* * *

And ever since, as I am told,
Gets it beforehand; and in gold.

Lord Calvin

Lord Calvin thought the Bishops should not sit
As Peers of Parliament.

And *argued* it!
In spite of which, for years, and years, and years,
They went on sitting with their fellow-peers.

Lord Henry Chase

What happened to Lord Henry Chase?
He got into a

                                           Libel Case!
The Daily Howl had said that he –
But could not prove it perfectly
To Judge or Jury's satisfaction:
His Lordship, therefore,

won the action.
But, as the damages were small,

He gave them to a Hospital.

Lord Heygate

LORD HEYGATE had a troubled face
His furniture was commonplace –
The sort of Peer who well might pass
For someone of the middle class.
I do not think you want to hear
About this unimportant Peer,
So let us leave him to discourse
About LORD EPSOM and his horse.

Lord Epsom

A Horse, Lord Epsom did bestride
With mastery and quiet pride.
He dug his spurs into its hide.

The Horse,

discerning it was pricked,

Incontinently

                 bucked and kicked,
A thing that no one could predict!

Lord Epsom clearly understood
The High-bred creature's nervous mood,

As only such a horseman could.

Dismounting,

       he was heard to say
That it was kinder to delay
His pleasure to a future day.

*   *   *

He had the Hunter led away.

Lord Finchley

Lord Finchley tried to mend the Electric Light
Himself.

It struck him dead: And serve him right!
It is the business of the wealthy man
To give employment to the artisan.

Lord Ali-Baba

Lord Ali-Baba was a Turk
Who hated every kind of work,
And would repose for hours at ease
With

       Houris seated on his knees.
A happy life! – Until, one day

Mossoo Alphonse Effendi Bey
(A Younger Turk: the very cream
And essence of the New Régime)
Dispelled this Oriental dream
By granting him a place at Court,

High Coffee-grinder to the Porte,
Unpaid: –

In which exalted Post
His Lordship yielded up the ghost.

Lord Hippo

Lord Hippo suffered fearful loss

By putting money on a horse
Which he believed, if it were pressed,
Would run far faster than the rest:
For

someone who was in the know

Had confidently told him so.

But

on the morning of the race

It only took

the *seventh* place!

Picture the Viscount's great surprise!
He scarcely could believe his eyes!

He sought the Individual who
Had laid him odds at 9 to 2,
Suggesting as a useful tip
That they should enter Partnership
And put to joint account the debt
Arising from his foolish bet.

But when the Bookie – oh! my word,
I only wish you could have heard
The way he roared he did not think,
And hoped that they might strike him pink!
Lord Hippo simply turned and ran
From this infuriated man.

Despairing, maddened and distraught
He utterly collapsed and sought
His sire,

the Earl of Potamus,
And brokenly addressed him thus:
"Dread Sire – to-day at Ascot – I …"
His genial parent made reply:
"Come! Come! Come! Come! Don't look so glum!
Trust your Papa and name the sum. …

. . . Fifteen hundred thousand? . . . Hum!
However . . . stiffen up, you wreck;
Boys will be boys – so here's the cheque!"
Lord Hippo, feeling deeply – well,
More grateful than he cared to tell –
Punted the lot on Little Nell:–
And got a telegram at dinner

To say

that he had backed the Winner!

Lord Uncle Tom

Lord Uncle Tom was different from
What other nobles are.
For they are yellow or pink, I think,
But he was  black as tar.

He had his father's debonair
  And rather easy pride:
But his complexion and his hair

Were from the mother's side.

He often mingled in debate
    And latterly displayed

Experience of peculiar weight
    Upon the Cocoa-trade.

But now he speaks no more.   The BILL
    Which he could not abide,
It preyed upon his mind until
    He sickened, paled, and died.

Lord Lucky

Lord Lucky, by a curious fluke,
Became a most important duke.
From living in a vile Hotel

A long way east of Camberwell

He rose in less than half an hour
To riches, dignity and power.
It happened in the following way:—
The Real Duke went out one day
To shoot with several people, one

Of whom had never used a gun.
This gentleman (a Mr. Meyer
Of Rabley Abbey, Rutlandshire),
As he was scrambling through the brake,

Discharged his weapon by mistake,
And plugged about an ounce of lead
Piff-bang into his Grace's Head—
Who naturally fell down dead.

His heir, Lord Ugly, roared, "You Brute!

Take that to teach you how to shoot!"
Whereat he volleyed left and right;
But being somewhat short of sight,
His right-hand Barrel only got
The second heir, Lord Poddleplot;
The while the left-hand charge (or choke)
Accounted for another bloke,
Who stood with an astounded air

Bewildered by the whole affair
– And was the third remaining heir.
After the

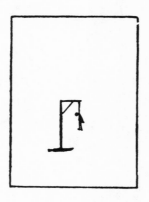

       Execution (which
Is something rare among the Rich)
Lord Lucky, while of course, he needed

Some

      help to prove his claim,
                           succeeded.
– But after his succession, though
All this was over years ago,
He only once indulged the whim
Of asking Meyer to lunch with him.

Lord Canton

The reason that

the present Lord Canton
Succeeded lately to his Brother John
Was that his Brother John, the elder son,
Died rather suddenly at forty-one.

The insolence of an Italian guide

Appears to be the reason that he died.

Lord Abbott

Lord Abbott's coronet was far too small,
So small, that as he sauntered down Whitehall
Even the youthful Proletariat
(Who probably mistook it for a Hat)
Remarked on its exiguous extent.

Here is a picture of the incident.

A MORAL ALPHABET

A

stands for

Archibald who told no lies,
And got this lovely volume for a prize.

The Upper School had combed and oiled their
    hair,
And all the Parents of the Boys were there.
In words that ring like thunder through the Hall,
Draw tears from some and loud applause from all, —

The Pedagogue, with Pardonable Joy,
Bestows the Gift upon the Radiant Boy: –

"Accept the Noblest Work produced as yet"
(Says he) "upon the English Alphabet;
"Next term I shall examine you, to find
"If you have read it thoroughly. So mind!"

And while the Boys and Parents cheered so loud,
That out of doors

a large and anxious crowd
Had gathered and was blocking up the street,
The admirable child resumed his seat.

MORAL

Learn from this justly irritating Youth,
To brush your Hair and Teeth and tell the Truth.

B stands for Bear.

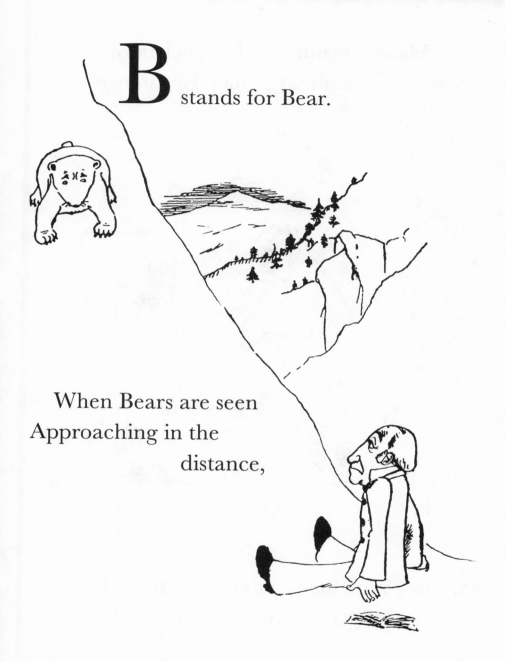

When Bears are seen
Approaching in the
       distance,

Make up your mind at once between
Retreat and Armed Resistance.

A Gentleman remained to fight –
With what result for him?

The Bear, with ill-concealed delight,
  Devoured him, Limb by Limb.

Another Person turned and ran;
  He ran extremely hard:
The Bear was faster than the Man,
  And beat him by a yard.

MORAL

Decisive action in the hour of need
Denotes the Hero, but does not succeed.

C stands for Cobra; when the Cobra

bites

An Indian Judge, the Judge spends restless nights.

MORAL

This creature, though disgusting and appalling,
Conveys no kind of Moral worth recalling.

D

The Dreadful

Dinotherium he
Will have to do his best for D.
The early world observed with awe
His back, indented like a saw.
His look was gay, his voice was strong;
His tail was neither short nor long;
His truck, or elongated nose,
Was not so large as some suppose;
His teeth, as all the world allows,
Were graminivorous, like a cow's.

He therefore should have wished to pass
Long peaceful nights upon the Grass,
But being mad the brute preferred
To roost in branches, like a bird.*
A creature heavier than a whale,
You see at once, could hardly fail
To suffer badly when he slid.

*We have good reason to suppose
 He did so, from his claw-like toes.

And tumbled

(as he always did).
His fossil, therefore, comes to light
All broken up: and serve him right.

MORAL
If you were born to walk the ground,
Remain there; do not fool around.

E

stands for

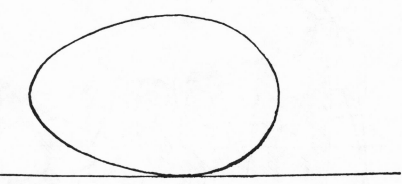

Egg.

MORAL
The Moral of this verse
Is applicable to the Young. Be terse.

F
for a

Family taking a walk
In Arcadia Terrace, no doubt:
The parents indulge in intelligent talk,
While the children they gambol about.

At a quarter-past six they return to their tea,
Of a kind that would hardly be tempting to me,
 Though my appetite passes belief.
There is Jam, Ginger Beer, Buttered Toast,
 Marmalade,
With Cold Leg of Mutton and Warm Lemonade,
And a large Pigeon Pie very skilfully made
 To consist almost wholly of Beef.

MORAL

A Respectable Family taking the air
 Is a subject on which I could dwell;
It contains all the morals that ever there were,
 And it sets an example as well.

G

stands for Gnu, whose weapons of Defence
Are long, sharp, curling Horns, and Common-
    sense,
To these he adds a Name so short and strong,

That even Hardy Boers pronounce it wrong.

How often on a bright Autumnal day
The Pious people of Pretoria say,
"Come, let us hunt the – " Then no more is heard
But Sounds of Strong Men struggling with a word.
Meanwhile, the distant Gnu with grateful eyes
Observes his opportunity, and flies.

MORAL

Child, if you have a rummy kind of name,
Remember to be thankful for the same.

H was a

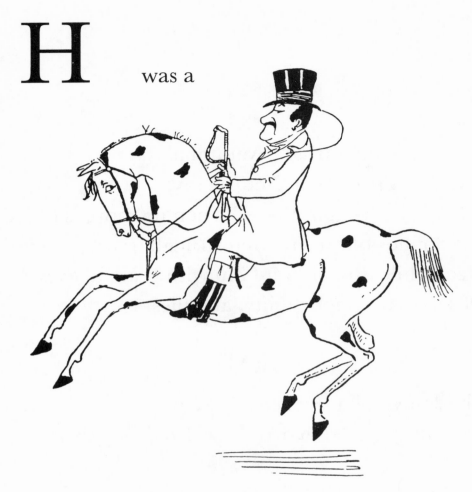

Horseman who rode to the meet,
And talked of the Pads of the fox as his "feet" –
An error which furnished subscribers with grounds
For refusing to make him a Master of Hounds.

He gave way thereupon to so fearful a rage,
That he sold up his Stable and went on the Stage,
And had all the success that a man could desire
In creating the Part of

"The Old English Squire."
MORAL

In the Learned Professions, a person should know
The advantage of having two strings to his bow.

I

the Poor Indian, justly called "The Poor,"

He has to eat his Dinner off the floor

MORAL

The Moral these delightful lines afford
Is: "Living cheaply is its own reward."

J stands for James, who thought it immaterial
  To pay his taxes, Local or Imperial.
  In vain the Mother wept, the Wife implored,
  James only yawned as though a trifle bored.

The Tax Collector called again, but he
Was met with Persiflage and Repartee.

When James was hauled before the learned Judge,
Who lectured him, he loudly whispered, "Fudge!"
The Judge was startled from his usual calm,
He

struck the desk before him with his palm,
And roared in tones to make the boldest quail,
"*J stands for James,* IT ALSO STANDS FOR JAIL."

And therefore, on a dark and dreadful day,
Policemen came and took him all away.

MORAL

The fate of James is typical, and shows
How little mercy people can expect
Who will not pay their taxes; (saving those
To which they conscientiously object).

K

for the Klondyke, a Country of Gold,
Where the winters are often excessively cold;
Where the lawn every morning is covered with
    rime,
And skating continues for years at a time.
Do you think that a Climate can conquer the grit
Of the Sons of the West? Not a bit! Not a bit!

When the weather looks nippy, the bold Pioneers
Put on two pairs of Stockings and cover their ears,
And roam through the drear Hyperborean dales
With a vast apparatus of Buckets and Pails;

Or wander through wild Hyperborean glades
With Hoes, Hammers, Pickaxes, Mattocks and
Spades.

There are some who give rise to exuberant mirth
By turning up nothing but bushels of earth,
While those who have little cause excellent fun
By attempting to pilfer from those who have none.
At times the reward they will get for their pains
Is to strike very tempting auriferous veins;
Or, a shaft being sunk for some miles in the
    ground,
Not infrequently nuggets of value are found.
They bring us the gold when their labours are
    ended,
And we – after thanking them prettily – spend it.

MORAL

Just you work for Humanity, never you mind
If Humanity seems to have left you behind.

L was a Lady, Advancing in Age,
    Who drove in her carriage and six,
With a Couple of Footmen, a Coachman and Page,
    Who were all of them regular bricks.

If the Coach ran away, or was smashed by a Dray,
    Or got into collisions and blocks,
The Page, with a courtesy rare for his years,
Would leap to the ground with inspiriting cheers,
While the Footman allayed her legitimate fears,
    And the Coachman sat tight on his box.

At night as they met round an excellent meal,
 They would take it in turn to observe:
"What a Lady indeed! . .what a presence to feel! . ."
"What a Woman to worship and serve! . . ."

But, perhaps, the most poignant of all their delights
 Was to stand in a rapturous Dream
When she spoke to them kindly on Saturday Nights
 And said "They deserved her Esteem."

MORAL

Now observe the Reward of these dutiful lives:
 At the end of their Loyal Career
They each had a Lodge at the end of the drives,
 And she left them a Hundred a Year.
Remember from this to be properly vexed
 When the newspaper editors say,
That "The type of society shown in the Text
 Is rapidly passing away."

M

was a Millionaire who sat at Table,
  And ate like this –

                    as long as he was able;
At half-past twelve the waiters turned him out:
  He lived impoverished and died of gout.

MORAL

Disgusting exhibition! Have a care
When, later on you are a Millionaire,
To rise from table feeling you could still
Take something more, and not be really ill.

N

stands for Ned, Maria's younger brother,

Who, walking one way, chose to gaze the other.

In Blandford Square – a crowded part of town –
Two people on a tandem knocked him down:

Whereat

a Motor Car, with warning shout
Ran right on top and turned him inside out:
The damages that he obtained from these
Maintained him all his life in cultured ease.

MORAL

The law protects you. Go your gentle way:
The Other Man has always got to Pay.

stands for Oxford. Hail! salubrious seat
Of learning! Academical Retreat!
Home of my Middle Age! Malarial Spot
Which People call Medeeval (though it's not).
The marshes in the neighbourhood can vie
With Cambridge, but the town itself is dry,
And serves to make a kind of Fold or Pen

Wherein to herd a lot of Learned Men.

Were I to write but half of what they know,
It would exhaust the space reserved for "O";
And, as my book must not be over big,
I turn at once to "P," which stands for Pig.

MORAL

Be taught by this to speak with moderation
Of places where, with decent application,
One gets a good, sound, middle-class education.

P

stands for Pig, as I remarked before,

A second cousin to the Huge Wild Boar.
But Pigs are civilised, while Huge Wild Boars

Live savagely, at random, out of doors,
And, in their coarse contempt for dainty foods,
Subsist on Truffles, which they find in woods.
Not so the cultivated Pig, who feels
The need of several courses at his meals,
But wrongly thinks it does not matter whether

He takes them one by one

or all together.
Hence, Pigs devour, from lack of self-respect,
What Epicures would certainly eject.

MORAL

Learn from the Pig to take whatever Fate
Or Elder Persons heap upon your plate.

Q

for Quinine, which children take

With Jam and little bits of cake.

MORAL

How idiotic! Can Quinine
Replace Cold Baths and Sound Hygiene?

R

the Reviewer,

reviewing my book,
At which he had barely intended to look;

But the very first lines upon "A" were enough
To convince him the *Verses* were excellent stuff.
So he wrote, without stopping, for several days
In terms of extreme but well-merited Praise.
To quote but one Passage: "No Person" (says he)
"Will be really content without purchasing three,
"While a Parent will send for a dozen or more,
"And strew them about on the Nursery Floor.
"The Versification might call for some strictures
"Were it not for its singular wit; while the
                                        Pictures,
"Tho' the handling of line is a little defective,
"Make up amply in *verve* what they lack in
                                        perspective."

MORAL

The habit of constantly telling the Truth
Will lend an additional lustre to Youth.

S

stands for Snail, who, though he be the least,
Is not an uninstructive Hornèd Beast.

His eyes are on his Horns, and when you shout
Or tickle them, the Horns go in and out.
Had Providence seen proper to endow
The furious Unicorn or sober Cow
With such a gift, the one would never now
Appear so commonplace on Coats of Arms.
And what a fortune for our failing farms
If circus managers, with wealth untold,
Would take the Cows for half their weight
                                    in gold!

MORAL

Learn from the Snail to take reproof with
                                    patience,
And not put out your Horns on all occasions.

T

for the Genial Tourist, who resides
In Peckham, where he writes Italian Guides.

MORAL

Learn from this information not to cavil
At slight mistakes in books on foreign travel.

U

for the Upas Tree,

that casts a blight
On those that pull their sisters' hair, and fight.

But oh! the Good! They wander undismayed.

And (as the Subtle Artist has portrayed)

Dispend the golden hours at play beneath its shade.*

   * A friend of mine, a Botanist, believes
     That Good can even browse upon its leaves.
     I doubt it. . . .

MORAL

Dear Reader, if you chance to catch a sight
Of Upas Trees, betake yourself to flight.

V for

the unobtrusive Volunteer,
Who fills the Armies of the World with fear.

MORAL

Seek with the Volunteer to put aside
The empty Pomp of Military Pride.

W

My little victim, let me trouble you
To fix your active mind on W.

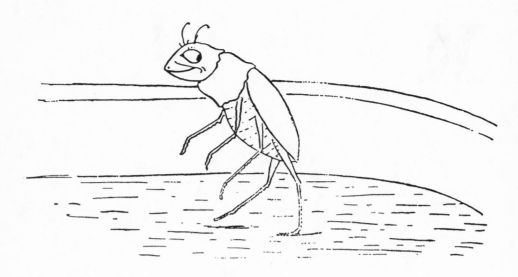

The WATERBEETLE here shall teach
A sermon far beyond your reach:
He flabbergasts the Human Race
By gliding on the water's face
With ease, celerity, and grace;
But if he ever stopped to think
Of how he did it, he would sink.

MORAL

Don't ask Questions!

No reasonable little Child expects
A Grown-up Man to make a rhyme on X.

MORAL

These verses teach a clever child to find
Excuse for doing all that he's inclined.

Y

stands for Youth (it would have stood for Yak,
But that I wrote about him two years back).
Youth is the pleasant springtime of our days,
As Dante so mellifluously says
(Who always speaks of Youth with proper praise).
You have not got to Youth, but when you do
You'll find what He and I have said is true.

MORAL

Youth's excellence should teach the Modern Wit
First to be Young, and then to boast of it.

Z

for this Zébu, who (like all Zebús)*
Is held divine by scrupulous Hindoos.

*Von Kettner writes it "Z_ebu"; Wurst "Zeb_u"
I split the difference and use the two.

MORAL

Idolatry, as you are aware,
Is highly reprehensible. But there,
We needn't bother – when we get to Z
Our interest in the Alphabet is dead.

LADIES
AND GENTLEMEN

I
The Garden Party

The Rich arrived in pairs
And also in Rolls Royces;

They talked of their affairs
In loud and strident voices.

(The Husbands and the Wives
Of this select society
Lead independent lives
Of infinite variety.)

The Poor arrived in Fords,
Whose features they resembled,

They laughed to see so many Lords
And Ladies all assembled.

The People in Between
Looked underdone and harassed,

And out of place and mean,
　　　And horribly embarrassed.

For the hoary social curse
Gets hoarier and hoarier,
And it stinks a trifle worse
Than in
The days of Queen Victoria,

when

They married and gave in marriage,
They danced at the County Ball,
And some of them kept a carriage.
AND THE FLOOD DESTROYED THEM ALL.

II
William Shand

There was a man called WILLIAM SHAND,
He had the habit of command,
And

    when subordinates would shout
He used to bang them all about.
It happened by a turn of Fate,
Himself became sub-ordinate,
Through being passenger upon
A liner, going to Ceylon.

One day, as they were in the Red
(Or Libyan) Sea,

the Captain
said:

"I think it's coming on to blow.
Let everybody go below!"
But William Shand said: "Not for me.
I'm going to stop on deck!" said he.
The Captain, wounded in his pride,
Summoned the Second Mate aside
And whispered: "Surely Mr. Shand
Must be extremely rich by land?"
"No," said the Mate, "when last ashore
I watched him. He is rather poor."

"Ho!" cried the Captain. "Stands it thus?
And shall the knave make mock of us?
I'll teach him to respect his betters.

Here, Bo'swain! Put the man in fetters!"

In fetters therefore
       William lay
Until the liner
       reached Bombay,

When he was handed to the court
Which deals with cases of the sort
In that uncomfortable port;
Which

promptly
 hanged him
  out of hand.

Such was the fate of William Shand.

MORAL
The moral is that people must,
If they are poor, obey or bust.

III

The Three Races

I

Behold, my child,
     the Nordic Man
And be as like
     him as you can.
His legs are long;
     his mind is slow;
His hair is lank
     and made of tow.

And here we have the Alpine Race.
Oh! What a broad and foolish face!

His skin is of a dirty yellow,
He is a most unpleasant fellow.

The most degraded of them all
Mediterranean we call.
His hair is crisp, and even curls,

And he is saucy with the girls.

IV
Obiter Dicta

I

SIR HENRY WAFFLE K.C. (*continuing*)

Sir Anthony Habberton, Justice and Knight,
Was enfeoffed of two acres of land

And it doesn't
    sound much

till you hear that the site
Was a strip to the South of the Strand.

HIS LORDSHIP (*Obiter Dictum*)

A strip to the South of the Strand
Is a good situation for land.

It is healthy and dry
And sufficiently high
And convenient on every hand.

II

SIR HENRY WAFFLE K.C. (*continuing*)

Now Sir Anthony, shooting in Timberley Wood,
Was imprudent enough to take cold;
And he

died without warning at six in the morning,
Because he was awfully old.

I have often been credibly told
That when people are awfully old
Though cigars are a curse

And

strong waters are worse

There is nothing so fatal as cold.

SIR HENRY WAFFLE K.C. (*continuing*)

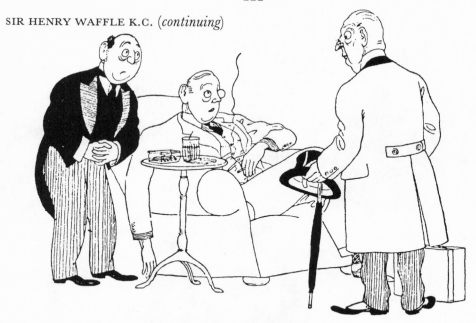

But Archibald answered on hearing the news: —
"I never move out till I must."
Which was all very jolly for *Cestui que Use*
But the Devil for *Cestui que Trust*.

HIS LORDSHIP (*Obiter Dictum*)

The office of *Cestui que Trust*
Is reserved for the learned and just.
Any villain you choose
May be *Cestui que Use*,
But a Lawyer for Cestui que Trust.

SIR HENRY WAFFLE K.C. (*continuing*)

Now the ruling laid down
in *Regina v. Brown*
May be cited. . . .

HIS LORDSHIP (*rising energetically*)

You're wrong!
It may not!

I've strained all
my powers
For some thirty-six hours
To unravel this pestilent rot.

THE WHOLE COURT (*rising and singing in chorus*)

Your Lordship is sound to the core.
It is nearly a quarter to four.

We've had quite enough
            Of this horrible stuff
And we don't want to hear any more!

LITTLE SILLY MAN (*rising at the back of the Court*)

Your Lordship is perfectly right.

He can't go on rhyming all night.
I suggest. . . .

(*He is gagged, bound and dragged off to a Dungeon.*)

V

The Statesman

I knew a man who used to say,
Not once but twenty times a day,

That in

the turmoil and the strife

(His very words) of Public Life

The thing of ultimate effect

Was Character –   not Intellect.

He therefore was at strenuous pains
To atrophy his puny brains
And registered success in this
Beyond the dreams of avarice,
Till, when he had at last become

Blind,

paralytic,

                         deaf and dumb,

Insensible and cretinous,
He was admitted
          ONE OF US.
They therefore, (meaning Them by "They")

His colleagues of the N.C.A.,

The T.U.C.,

the I.L.P.

Appointed him triumphantly
To bleed the taxes of a clear
200,000 Francs a year
(Swiss),

as the necessary man

For

Conferences at Lausanne,
Geneva, Basle, Locarno, Berne:

A salary which he will earn,
Yes – *earn* I say –

until he Pops,

Croaks, passes in his checks and Stops: –

When he will be remembered for
A week, a month, or even more.

VI

The Author

There is a literary man,
Whose name is

Herbert Keanes:
His coat is lined with astrachan.
He lives on private means.

His house is in St. James's Square
(Which I could not afford).
His head is strong but short of hair,
His Uncle is a Lord.

This Uncle loves him
       like a son

And has been heard to vow
He will be famous later on
And even might be now.

And he has left him in his will
New Boyton, Hatton Strand,
Long Stokely, Pilly-on-the-Hill,
And Lower Sandiland.

He is not dead, but when he dies
This wealth will all accrue,
Unless the old gafoozler lies,
O Herbert Keanes, to you!

The Son? The Son whom *She* alone
Could bear to such a sire,
The son of Lady Jane O'Hone
And Henry Keanes Esquire.

First with a private tutor, then
At Eton Herbert Keanes,
Like other strong successful men
Was nurtured in his teens.

To curious dons he next would pay
His trifling entrance fee,

And was accepted, strange to say,
By those of Trinity:

Tall Trinity whereby the Cam
Its awful torrent rolls,
But there! – I do not care a damn,
It might have been All Souls.

Has sat for Putticombe in Kent
But lost the seat he won

By boldly saying what he meant
Though meaning he had none.

Has written "Problems of the Poor,"

"The Future
of Japan"

And "Musings by
Killarney's Shore"

And

"What Indeed
is Man?"

And

"Flowers and Fruit"
(a book of verse)

"The Ethics
of
St. Paul,"

"Was there a Peter?"
(rather worse)

And

"Nero"
(worst of all).

Clubs: Handy Dandy, Beagle's, Tree's, Pitt, Palmerston, Riviere,

The Walnut Box, Empedocles,

Throgmorton, Pot o' Beer.

(The last for its bohemian lists
Wherein he often meets
Old Wasters,

Poets,

Communists,

And Ladies from the Streets.)

A strong Protectionist, believes
In everything but Heaven.
For entertainment, dines, receives,
Unmarried, 57.

The Example

John Henderson, an unbeliever,
Had lately lost his Joie de Vivre
From reading far too many books.
He went about with gloomy looks;
Despair inhabited his breast
And made the man a perfect pest.
Not so his sister, Mary Lunn,
She had a whacking lot of fun!
Though unbelieving as a beast
She didn't worry in the least.

But drank as hard as she was able

And sang and danced upon the table;

And

when she met her brother Jack

She used to smack him on the back
So smartly as to make him jump,
And cry, "What-ho! You've got the hump!"
A phrase which, more than any other,
Was gall and wormwood to her brother;
For, having an agnostic mind,
He was exceedingly refined.

The Christians, a declining band,
Would point with monitory hand

To Henderson his desperation,
To Mary Lunn her dissipation,
And often mutter, "Mark my words!
Something will happen to those birds!"

Which came to pass: for

Mary Lunn
Died suddenly, at ninety-one,

Of Psittacosis, not before
Becoming an appalling bore.
While Henderson, I'm glad to state,
Though naturally celibate,
Married an intellectual wife
Who made him lead the Higher life

And

wouldn't give him any wine;
Whereby he fell in a decline,
And, at the time of writing this,
Is suffering from paralysis,
The which, we hear with no surprise,
Will shortly end in his demise.

MORAL

The moral is (it is indeed!)
You mustn't monkey with the Creed.

HILAIRE BELLOC (1870–1953) was born in France during a thunderstorm. His life was tempestuous: his great intellect, evident from an early age, and his violent energy made him restless and demanding, needing constant company and never spending more than a few months in the same place. His French father died when he was two and his English mother brought him up in Sussex. A zealous Roman Catholic, he was educated at Cardinal Newman's Oratory School in Birmingham. He took a first-class degree in History at Balliol College, Oxford, but he failed to win a Fellowship at All Souls' and never forgot this bitter disappointment. At nineteen he fell in love with an American, Elodie Hogan, and married her in 1896. They had five children who grew up with Elodie at King's Land, a rambling house near West Grinstead likened by one shocked visitor to a 'gypsy encampment'. When Elodie died in 1914, Belloc went into permanent mourning, wearing black for the rest of his life and kissing her locked bedroom door whenever he passed it.

Apart from a brief period (1906–10) as Liberal M.P. for Salford, Belloc travelled and worked as a freelance writer and journalist, producing essays, articles, novels, books of travel and biography, poetry and verses in quantity and at great speed. He published over 150 prose works of history, political and economic theory, and religious apologetics, but nearly all are now forgotten and he is remembered for certain much-loved poems and his comic verse for children. All his wit and technical command of language are displayed in his *Cautionary Verses,* in which he made fun of the 'Awful Warning' lessons offered to the young in the early nineteenth century.

B. T. B. – Basil Temple Blackwood (1870–1917) was Hilaire Belloc's exact contemporary and met him when they were both undergraduates at Balliol College, Oxford. The third son of the first Marquess of Dufferin and Ava, Blackwood – unlike Belloc – was a Protestant and a High Tory, but the two men became close friends. They shared a sense of the ridiculous and Blackwood illustrated many of Belloc's books, the first being *The Bad Child's Book of Beasts* (1896), begun when the two friends went on holiday to Scandinavia in 1895. Untrained as an artist, Blackwood's considerable reputation as a comic draughtsman is based solely on his drawings in Belloc's work, for he published little else. By the time Belloc wrote *Cautionary Tales for Children* in 1906 Blackwood was working as a colonial civil servant in the Government Offices in Bloemfontein in South Africa, but their perfect collaboration was not disturbed by operating at a distance.

When World War I began in 1914, Blackwood joined the Grenadier Guards and was killed in action three years later.

Nicolas Clerihew Bentley (1907–78) was the son of the novelist E. C. Bentley, the inventor of the four-line comic rhyme known as the 'clerihew'. His godfather was G.K. Chesterton, a close friend of Hilaire Belloc. Nicolas studied drawing at Heatherley's School of Art and after a brief period of work as a circus clown and a film extra in 1927 he joined Shell's publicity office, where he drew humorous advertisements. In 1930 he decided to go freelance and one of his first commissions was to illustrate Belloc's *New Cautionary Tales*, with which he proved himself the ideal successor to B. T. B. and established a reputation for witty and stylish work. He went on to illustrate over seventy books, including T. S. Eliot's *Old Possum's Book of Practical Cats*, as well as regularly contributing pocket cartoons to the *Daily Mail* and the *Sunday Telegraph* and writing historical thrillers. He became a director of the publishing firm of André Deutsch in 1950.

DANIEL DEFOE *Robinson Crusoe*
Illustrated by W. J. Linton and others

CHARLES DICKENS *A Christmas Carol*
Illustrated by Arthur Rackham

SIR ARTHUR CONAN DOYLE *Sherlock Holmes*
Illustrated by Sidney Paget

C. S. EVANS *Cinderella*
The Sleeping Beauty
Illustrated by Arthur Rackham

OLIVER GOLDSMITH, WILLIAM COWPER and OTHERS
Ride a-Cock-Horse and other
Rhymes and Stories
Illustrated by Randolph Caldecott

KENNETH GRAHAME *The Wind in the Willows*
Illustrated by Arthur Rackham

THE BROTHERS GRIMM *Fairy Tales*
Illustrated by Arthur Rackham

NATHANIEL HAWTHORNE *A Wonder-Book*
Illustrated by Arthur Rackham

FRANCES HODGSON BURNETT *The Secret Garden*
Illustrated by Charles Robinson

Little Lord Fauntleroy
Illustrated by C. E. Brock

JOSEPH JACOBS *English Fairy Tales*
Illustrated by John Batten

WALTER JERROLD *Mother Goose's Nursery Rhymes*
Illustrated by Charles Robinson

RUDYARD KIPLING *The Jungle Book*
Illustrated by Kurt Wiese

Just So Stories
Illustrated by the Author

ROGER LANCELYN GREEN *The Adventures of Robin Hood*
Illustrated by Walter Crane

King Arthur and his Knights
of the Round Table
Illustrated by Aubrey Beardsley

EDWARD LEAR *A Book of Nonsense*
Illustrated by the Author

GEORGE MACDONALD *The Princess and the Goblin*
Illustrated by Arthur Hughes

L. M. MONTGOMERY *Anne of Green Gables*
Illustrated by Sybil Tawse

E. NESBIT *The Railway Children*
Illustrated by C. E. Brock

CHARLES PERRAULT *Little Red*
Riding Hood and other Stories
Illustrated by W. Heath Robinson

ANNA SEWELL *Black Beauty*
Illustrated by Lucy Kemp-Welch

ROBERT LOUIS STEVENSON *A Child's Garden of Verses*
Illustrated by Charles Robinson

Kidnapped
Illustrated by Rowland Hilder

Treasure Island
Illustrated by Mervyn Peake

JEAN WEBSTER *Daddy-Long-Legs*
Illustrated by the Author

OSCAR WILDE *The Happy Prince and*
other Tales
Illustrated by Charles Robinson

JOHANN WYSS *The Swiss Family Robinson*
Illustrated by Louis Rhead